Amma's Gospel

FOREWORD P C K Prem
ART Niloufer Wadia
CONCEPT Meera Chowdhry

POETRY Rajender Krishan

D1502539

Amma's Gospel

By

Rajender Krishan Chowdhry

Setu Publications
* Pittsburgh, PA (USA) *

© Rajender Krishan Chowdhry,
NY 11364, USA; rk@boloji.net

All illustrations in this book
© Niloufer Wadia, Pune, India.

We would be pleased to receive email correspondence regarding this publication or related topics at setuedit@gmail.com.

ISBN-13 (paperback): 978-1-947403-11-6
Paperback, 168 pages, US$ 14.95
Distributed to the book trade worldwide by Setu Publications, USA

Setu Literary Publications, Pittsburgh, USA

For

Isha, Jiya,
Siddharth and Samarth

With love and affection
from Grandpa

About the Book

Amma's Gospel is not only a medium of illumination but also an expression of civilizational and cultural foundation the poet wishes to convey, and so builds up a lyrical edifice to confirm.

Rajender Krishan tries to capture the spirit of age through the eyes and words and the innocuous counsels of worldly-wise knowledge and insight of old *ma – Amma ji*. It is about man's indistinct religious, social and intellectual affiliations, and human bondages belonging to discrete mental and rational regions where the old woman enters so often and gives discourse in fragments of judgment with isolated serious reflections on man's real worth in creating a world of peace and harmony with an attitude of total surrender of ego to humility.

Mother is never an individual but a collective symbol of harmony and sorority. She is the quintessence of patience, tolerance and love for humankind and perhaps, ultimately, stands before each one to say that to love man is to love 'the self and humanity' and thus, a restrained and yet so obvious yearning to establish peace and harmony in a not very healthy age.

Table of Contents

List of Poems

List of Poems

Foreword

'*Om*' is a sacred and spiritual sound recognized as the timbre of the universe. *Om*, the essence of ultimate reality unites all existing creations in the world. Insignia and echo alleviate disquieting thoughts and convey import of cosmic love and unity. If one delves deep it symbolizes '*Atman*, the soul, the self' *Brahma*, the Ultimate Reality. It speaks of the extraterrestrial principle of existence and wisdom even as the 'salutation' is the most pertinent beginning of such comforting lyrics of timeless values that lead to the heart and mind of *Amma*, the eternal foundation of love and inspiration.

Om
Primordial energy
The sound of silence

Om
The Only Verse
Manifesting eternally
The Universe

From a mystifying but evocative voyage to the 'inside' of man through incantation of '*Om*' and salutation to 'the inner' man,' it is a heartrending and nostalgic cruise to past unfathomed. Meditation on *'Om'* is a solemn yearning to enjoy life in the land of *Brahma.*

The poet with an anguished psyche evokes days of unfortunate partition (1947 India) when many lost mother country and turned refugees. He is beholden to the instinctive wisdom, patience and fortitude of *'Amma ji'*, who simply beseeches lord's blessings and prays, but shows ignorance lest the children should feel grief-stricken. It appears deliberate so that the children do not peek into troubled mind because security of lineage is very important for the old woman. *Amma* – a symbol of endurance and resilience always expresses quiet gratitude to Him ...that He saved life of the entire clan.

> *"I don't know"*,
> yet placing her hand on her chest
> she would assert confidently:
> *"The One that is always with me*
> *Have no doubt, That One Knows"*

History of humankind in distress, it is that reveals man's adversities amidst widespread suffering and uncertainty, he tells subtly. Perhaps for many survivors, it resurrects a threatening chapter in the life of humanity they never want to revisit but unsuspectingly continue to run through and feel skeptical or embittered.

To know the spirit of *'Namaste'* or folded hands – Greetings, it is 'Salutations to the One/ That pervades the entire Cosmos' an Indian way to hail, acknowledge and bear out obeisance and reverence to not only the man but also it is recognition of lord's presence in everyone, a sign of humility and geniality.

> Conveying gratitude
> With a pleasing attitude
> You merely don't greet
> …
> To the Witness
> That pervades all.

'Simran' indicates 'keeping in mind the Supreme Truth, the spiritual Person of 'the self', a man often disregards. It is tribute to inner strength – indicative of spiritual power because the Supreme Spirit, the Ancient Person lives in everyone. Poet in him not only reminds of the delusory potency - *Maya* (*Leela*) of the Supreme, who lives in everybody's heart but also tells man that if he treasures the Eternal Spirit, he is nearer to god. Lord's *Leela* (the delusory frolics) is just to

11

entertain, and then to reinvigorate devotees' faith. The mysterious and yet obvious expansion in existential situation is the usual but definite pastime the Absolute, the controller of the universe indulges in to edify man.

> Who is in control
> of this phenomenon?
> The Master Puppeteer! …
> always within
> from birth to death

That one ought to be true to 'the self' should be the true and candid pathway to arrive at the objective. The sacrosanct pursuit will not engage 'the inner man' in any ineffectual context life once cherished, for it would turn into an unqualified waste.

> The sham and deviousness
> of playing blame games
> makes you a gadget of ego
> that traps and ensnares
> leading to a fraudulent integrity
> (*Amma*'s Gospel)

Dishonesty does not permit man to see his own face, and therefore, fails to listen to the inner voice.

To avoid rational outlook even if temporarily, attains wisdom, physical and spiritual health and accepts one's folly, is equal to yearning for lord's grace. An act of gratitude it is not only to 'the self', who is at times 'the inner controller but also to Him who exists in everything and still stands at a distance and separate as if not an active participant. Live life as it comes, and you are rich. Determination and sturdiness give strength to endure obstructions. To keep good health, quality of equity, righteousness and humility is lord's Grace. Hate greed and strive for riches of the soul and you get what you deserve.

'Why Pray – Love' is the principle motivating force. *'Amma'* advises to observe restraint on desires, feelings and words, and counsels to stay away from negative thoughts

> You get what you deserve
> Only when it becomes due

A man underscores the eternal truth but deliberately avoids accepting, for he is obsessive and is attached to worldly life and enjoys experiencing its transitory character notwithstanding wisdom of the lord and his *maya* – the delusory potency (Cyclical). 'Birth, death and rebirth' is not in the hand of man. *Prakriti* (the mode of three *gunas)* and *Purusha* continue to guide man's destiny. Under the spell of *prakriti* even lord permits freedom to human beings to cultivate *sattva, rajas* and *tamas gunas* and thereafter, direct providence and at this stage, the lord expands range of options a man ought to make.

A big question of salvation haunts every individual. However, even scriptures fail to satisfy man's quest. To understand the phenomenon of cycle of birth and death, know the distance in time between the heartbeats, which is a real dilemma defying rationalization.

Infinitesimal rotations shield the mystery of birth and death that an intrusive man experiences without expounding its embryonic meaning. Life's mystery is a grand spectacle known and still ambiguous. Life is meditation on the unknown, the Supreme Lord who is close and yet far off, for to comprehend divine potency and its deluding frisks is complex. You become an eyewitness and enjoy and at that moment, questions disturb a probing mind about the riddle that birth, death and rebirth will go down the abyss of infinitely deep quietness.

Rajender Krishan's anxieties amaze as he tries to split up its multiple regions where each one mixes up to confound.

14

As he confronts chaotic psychosomatic structure, he goes to *Amma ji*. In fact, *Amma* reveals the ultimate truth of the Great Spirit, the lord, the Supreme Person, the protector of living beings and his eternal delusory prowess that continues through all ages and *Manavantaras* and guards its devotees while reprimanding the evil doers. *Amma*, in wholesomeness, innocence and simulated nescience speaks of the ever-fresh delusory energy at work. She assumes the most benign figure of 'mother of humankind' one begins to realize and so the poet if immortalizes '*Amma*' it is for wellbeing of humanity. To the mysterious 'cycle' of life, *Amma* provides a modest smile – a comforting stroke.

> The cycle
> of physical birth and death
>
> ...Such is the game plan
> of *Prakriti* and *Purusha*
> that innumerable civilizations
> have come and gone
> and man is still wandering
> here, there, everywhere
> in understanding
> the greater cycle of Nature.
> (Cyclical)

The eternal 'Quest' to find the essence of the cycle of births and deaths continues. Is it play of delusory power of the great lord or some invisible hand in the backdrop? Man fails and still expects to find resolution to the issue of birth and death even while the intellectual pursuits imperceptibly continue. What is the 'cosmic intelligence' that often disturbs? Deliverance is freedom from anxieties to know about death and life before death and after.

No one precisely understands the numinous phenomenon despite knowledge of Holy Scriptures. *Amma* is straight when she says, 'you love, be honest' and there is 'Nothing more to know/ Nothing to gain, nothing to Lose.' Arguments will be interminable and ultimately, the concept of 'absolute Reality' will linger on as a mystery within reach and still far off. Genuine 'Silence' of unsteady mind means the inability to reach the Unknown Truth or it could be otherwise if one can determine its intensity and enormity.

What is this phenomenon
of recurring births and deaths
that the Scriptures talk about?
What is Salvation?

16

'Word' is the key to understanding the entire mystery of life, its origin, objective and the eventual destination, only than one comprehends its varied meanings and shades of connotation. It is the primary input to the door of supremely divine land.

> get the key to unlock
> the supreme potential within,
> that encapsulates
> the absolute existence

'Amma' is an embodiment of relations of varied nature. It brings pride if a child goes beyond what parents think, learns to forgive, knows the ultimate reality the death, and waits for a new life … deliverance, and further suggests modestly to share life's delight, for life is a blessing. Never permit whatever is acrimonious or harsh to enter home she often tells discreetly.

> *Amma*'s spirituality:
> Love yourself immensely…

> *Amma*'s mysticism:
> Death is inevitable
> sleep with gratitude
> for the ultimate dawn

Current age is difficult, anxious and dreadful, as corona makes lives awesome. It only signals death and destruction (Healing) with a fractured hope. In moments of crisis, a man goes to *Amma* with obvious cravings so that he finds inner solace. A simple counsel is to confront the predictable death and possible challenges, and practice self-control when *Yama* stands before you.

> Know and follow *Yam*
> the *Patanjali sutras*
> of self-control

To reach 'Destination' of life, father is purely a guide not the objective. Emulation is possible but non-natural endeavor takes a man nowhere. He again hints at the understated destination an individual soul ought to reach. It is to merge with the absolute, the ultimate Reality. It is a feeling of total silence and tranquility when one feels liberated from the manacles and shield of 'the self' called body. One wanders freely sans restrictions and bondages, which is a path to final deliverance.

> The destination
> always is emancipation
> of the Self.

Father guides on the right path but it is not the purpose. If path is for growth and progress discard the old. Imposition is not advisable. Helping hand of love and motivation matters and is a way to true independence. Parenting changes and takes one to destination. It is a path to liberation of 'the self'. A feeling of composure and self-assurance saves from embarrassment and traumatic delusions. Here, '*Shiva*' is an image of equilibrium in totally contrasting situations, but it symbolizes divine union.

Observe patience with total humility and love, as the 'The Present' spreads out in abundance before you and imagine that it delineates clear margins and flexibility of Time, Space and Causation. It is god's gift and therefore, a man ought to experience this moment as Eternity.

Transcend the limits;
eliminate the shadows
and experience
Now as Eternity...

Beyond delusion is the reality, find it, for on this side, you live and on the other side of entryway, resides the Supreme. Get rid of illusory world he urges, and merge with the ultimate reality, the supreme and this way, the man will be on the path of self-realization and the eternal truth. To dissolve in the infinite – the Primordial Energy, the Supreme Truth is the goal. Man's destination is intimation of a search for the 'swinging grandeur of life' and 'an engaging riddle' to hang around as a seeker (Unpredictable). It is man's future for it will lead him to true redemption – *mukti* and that way he knows the 'One - Primordial Energy - Supreme Truth.'

> The Guru will destroy
> your most precious possession
> – the Ego
> (*Gurdwara*)

A person is really a Karma yogi (Impetus), who throws aside obstacles and acts as a mechanism to motivate and confront challenges and so overcome hardships. If one scrutinizes the thought pattern of Amma, firmness to fight against challenges is discernible.

> Those responsible
> for elbowing…
> are in fact God sent catalysts,
> steadily triggering
> the sparks of motivation

To know the ways of life of a mystic teaches art of life, its wisdom, victory, dynamism and detachment, and final attainment - the realization.

Awesome
is the experience
once the mindful
grasps the proximity
to the destination
(Steps)

Every 'step' a man takes in life ought to be charismatic and majestic and must reflect on the integrity of man, and it will be fit to encounter any challenge.

'Life' is empty this moment and it is full of meaning the next minute. If a man comprehends its mystery and eternal elasticity of transformation, it not only gives joy but also leads to reminiscent essence sans any philosophic connotations. Life hides enigma in its purity and simplicity.

… and
notwithstanding the inferences
Life - the eternal mystic
moves on
with its own conundrum…

of vagaries and variables.
(Life)

The ultimate truth is the experience in aloneness. When he talks of the five elements – the earth, the water, the fire, the air and the ether, it points out at fathomless pursuits manifest in life force that disintegrates. Nothing exists without the elements, and its composition is a transitory spectacle.

Anything that can be
seen and touched
is a mere configuration
of the elements five
(Transient)

Elements are eternal. One may bury or burn the forms these espouse but soon, these fall apart and then, come back to original eternal form. Body's functions are perishable, but the elements are long-lasting. In most of the lyrics a philosophic current flow, which at times, is noticeable and then ingeniously it speaks of imminent collapse of life. As a devastating thinker he even goes beyond but an ordinary human being thinks of imminent hazards. Everyone in whatever stage of life finds adequate justifications to stay away from confronting the predicament and probably it results

22

in capitalizing on the crisis. In fact, solution to the problem is to *'Don't talk, just do it'* now and here defying impossibilities.

To cast off avarice teaches art of life. He speaks of five elements and confirms consciousness of the perpetually ordained conflict and ability to stay independent and so these do not lead to any enduring construction (Independence) but 'blending and merger' is evocative creative process.

Surrender in all humility
to the Witness within
the only Sovereign,
unperturbed and carefree
as the eternal concept
of independence

Nothing is sturdy on earth. Undergoing transformation elevates, purifies and teaches life differently or it is exhibit of unsightly visage of humankind (Observation). Only rational outlook is absent as exploitation and tyranny continue to 'to desecrate the *Garden of Eden'* in the name of One *unknown* God' one believes.

Since time immemorial, it happens, even fiends preach morality in the battlefield and so, the ageless questions mystify.

One questions if there is something
more disgraceful known to mankind,
besides the cruel and beastly instincts?
(Observation)

In united endeavor despite transitory
breakdown, man ought to imbibe habit of sustained
efforts, explore and feel the delight of living in
unity. Underneath, the thought of reflection inspires
even as 'Exploitation' opens eyes of intellectuals to
the real play that powers-that-be indulge in and
hoodwink public, and still sermonize on truth,
justice and compassion amidst growling poverty
and deprivation. A struggle to control time, space
and causation continues as the questions of 'thine
and mine' the disintegrating forces stay whereas
materialism appears invasive causing violence and
hatred.

If wise men call life as a construction of *maya*
– the delusory potency of the Invisible and ignore
'the primordial shine' it is a mirage where the 'no-
win' situation persists while, 'It struggles to
discover /The Truth of "*Thine*" and "*Mine*", which
appears an elementary requisite.

To pray and worship is to attain peace. It is
an encounter with a mystic, who teaches art of
living a disconnected life (Leaf). It makes it good,

but a man never gets genuine peace of mind, for he knows, ultimately life is nothing but a waste, a fistful of dust that dissolves into earth. Nonetheless, the question stares at the intangible quintessence whether it is transformation or liberation or what you call *Nirvana* - a free life hereafter.

> Is this dissolution
> Death or Life?
> Perhaps,
> The path that we seek
> ... *Nirvana*

'Detachment' is a state of mind when one is cut off from the outside world. Truly one finds the world and the creator in 'the self', an image of god. Frequent glimpses of the Supreme and *Amma's* Gospel in the verses of Rajender Krishan are the strength in a world of crisis where intolerance, nervousness, constricted consciousness, tedium and apathy govern. Capacity to 'disconnect' from outside world is an alleyway to the land of supreme bliss, 'Serenity' he calls in some verses.

> Detachment is
> the ability to switch off…
> from any action and simply be

with the self within...
for the *Karmic* dynamism
needs to remain carefree

The expression '*Karmic* dynamism' alerts man to be cautious, for the three *gunas* – the modes of *prakriti* when unite with *purusha*, determine the course of destiny and so he tells that if *karmas* are genuine and bereft of sinful intents, man is at peace with 'the self' and it is a testimonial of 'god's existence in man.

The poet invokes the principle of *karma* for a virtuous and objective life, for its fruit visits the doer. In *Karmas*, the three *gunas* – the modes *Prakriti* work actively to determine man's truth, purity and uprightness (*Sattvic*), passion or infatuation or energy (*Rajas*) and lethargy or iniquity (*Tamas*) nature of man.

The inside of man is manifestation of harmony and distress depending up the psychological approach and characteristics. Man's outlook on life should eschew absurdity to react resolutely.

Both heaven and hell
are echoes and images
revealing the temperament

of one's own persona
(Heaven and Hell)

In the identical element of wisdom, he epigrammatically describes the true meaning of (Guilt). A man confronts 'the self', when iniquity, acts of conquest and tyranny, mortify 'equanimity' and *Amma's* counsels work wonder, who (in Repudiation) says innocently, *"Renounce deceit / Shun crookedness."*

Lyrical discourse goads intellects to serious deliberations on life and death, whereas virtue confers definiteness, and to deliberate on life with a constructive attitude is good. Otherwise, it grows into a farce if you talk of fractional evolution when as tiny insects' ants symbolize a little impediment. Find solution or else you meet defeat he affirms. A man may encounter contrary situations in life (Purpose), but efforts ought to continue to reach objective where 'karmic seeds' of *sattvic* nature are conducive to the realization of true meaning of life.

For everyone, it is a journey to 'the inside' of man, whose finger the ever eternal *'Amma'* holds and takes him to a life of love, compassion, harmony and divine bliss in times of catastrophe.

Lyrics are 'Tributes to Amma'... the first word a child utters and so dies with it...

Amma exists in everyone whether visible or invisible as if she is the Supreme, he reminds and it makes the anthology intimate, unforgettable and unique.

P C K Prem
October 2020

Acknowledgements

Amma's Gospel would not have materialized without the support of my beloved wife for 45 years, **Meera Chowdhry** – an alumnus of Miranda College, who has always been the first to read and reflect to whatever gets written by me. She is a pillar of strength rendering much need support to everyone in the family.

My gratitude to **Mr. P C K Prem** for writing the foreword to this book. Prem ji (P C Katoch of Garh-malkher, Palampur, HP, a former academician, civil servant and member of Himachal Public Service Commission, Shimla), a triangular author of several books and a post-graduate (1970) in English literature from Punjab University, Chandigarh, is a poet, novelist, short story writer, translator and a critic in English from Himachal Pradesh.

Niloufer Wadia who has interpreted each and every poem in this book with illustrations, after having spent over 20 years in advertising, quit to follow her first loves, fine art and illustration. She paints in acrylics and watercolors, and illustrates in a wide variety of styles, from children's picture books to medical tomes, in the traditional and digital media.

And finally, my gratitude to Dr. Rama Rao Vadapalli, VB, Dr. S. Padmapriya, PhD, Professor. Satya Chaitanya, Sunil Sharma, Neera Pradhan, Dr. Jaipal Singh, Simi Nallaseth, Dr. Amitabh Mitra, Rajiv Khandelwal and Bhupinder Singh, for kindly previewing the book. The previews are appended at the end of the book.

Rajender Krishan
October 27, 2020

Preface

As has been my wont, whenever I am confronted with dilemma, I end up invoking *Amma* (my paternal grandma – Shrimati Ratan Devi: 1900-1982). I invariably get answers to the questions and also her guidance to deal with the difficult situations in life. As a humble tribute, this collection contains several poems where I have reflectively reminisced Amma, in an attempt to appreciate her fond memories and seeking her forever relevant guidance.

In reverence!

Rajender Krishan
October 27, 2020

Om

Om
Primordial energy
The sound of silence

Om
The Only Verse
Manifesting eternally
The Universe

Namaste

Salutations to the One
That pervades the entire Cosmos

As I honor that space in thee
Where dwells
The very Cause of Life
Unanimously
We hear together
The symphony playing the notes
Of love, light, truth, harmony
In our throbbing hearts' solitude
Vibrating and enriching
Humility, compassion, fortitude

Amma ji

Amma, had faced the colonial
subjugation and suppression;
finally gained independence
only to become a refugee,
a migrant in her *own* country
in the post-partitioned India

Yet all these drastic transitions,
could not shake her verve for life
Amma led her entire clan
with patience and resilience
by simply being and doing
whatever was required to be done

Amma knew her limitations, often
admitting by saying "*I don't know*",
yet placing her hand on her chest
she would assert confidently:
"*The One that is always with me
Have no doubt, That One Knows*"

Lighting the *diya* for the daily *Aarti*
Offering gratitude, seeking fortitude
Amma would engrave in our ambience
the Principle, that transforms even today
into a blessed and enthralling epoch
each time she walks down my memory lane.

Greetings

***Amma* always said:**

Every time whoever you meet
Remember to always greet
With a smiling face
And folded hands

I would argue:

All I need to do is say *"Hi"*
So, doing all those gestures
Why?

She would lovingly explain:

Beware
Rather Be Aware
Every time you say,
Namaste

Working as an *aide-memoire*
It awakens you from stupor
to experience and realize
that in every organism alive
The Witness reclines
in the temple divine

Conveying gratitude
With a pleasing attitude
You merely do not greet
Every big and small
Essentially you bow
To the Witness
That pervades all.

When will I learn?

Love yourself
by being true to yourself
Be not in haste to react
First anticipate then contemplate
and
then respond
Follow the right path
Be happy
Be successful.

Leela*

Conscious of being alive
is being cognizant of breathing
that happens without volition
    — akin to a *Simran*** —
in a well-defined order
in every living organism.

Who is in control of this phenomenon?
The Master Puppeteer!
Invisible and mysterious,
    as if nowhere,
    while effectively being *now here*,
always within
from birth to death

warranting yet,
the cosmos of Life
    — in this eternal *Leela* —
wanders *ad infinitum*
in search of the miraculous
here, there, and everywhere.

* *Leela* = play
** *Simran* derived from *smarana* in Sanskrit means the act of
continuous remembrance of the spiritual and higher aspects of
the self.

Amma's Gospel

Amma's gospel was simple:

Love yourself
by being true to yourself
Be not in haste to react
First anticipate then contemplate
and
then respond
Follow the right path
Be happy
Be successful.

I would express my curiosity

Amma would elaborate:

Stop electing
the path of deceit
in the journey of life
The path of deceitfulness
makes you the key contestant
against your very own self
while cruising through
the vagaries and variables
in the play of life

This play of deception
sets up boundaries
to make you
a prisoner of the past
that has long been dead
yet keeps haunting
And you simply keep longing
to be free from the bondages

Treacherous is this play
that hoodwinks you to become
a puppet of emotions
a victim of desires
and not the master of your mind

The sham and deviousness
of playing blame games
makes you a gadget of ego
that traps and ensnares
leading to a fraudulent integrity
of tumbling self-esteem
unable to see its very own reflection

What is the way then, I would ask?

Amma **would respond:**

Love yourself
by being true to yourself
Be not in haste to react
First anticipate then contemplate
and
then respond
Follow the right path
Be happy
Be successful.

~*~

Have I fathomed?

Why Pray?

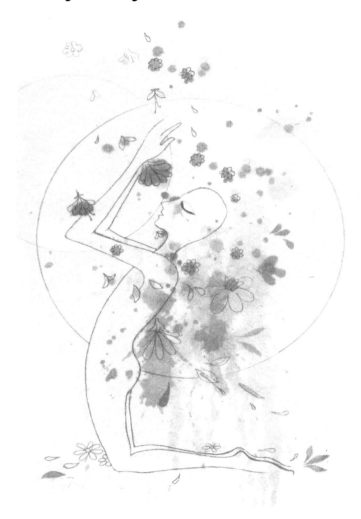

***Amma* would often say:**

Always Pray

How to pray? I would ask

***Amma* would explain:**

As a seeker, accepting ignorance
In helplessness, reasoning
   mortals cannot do everything
For knowledge to train for physical,
   psychic and spiritual health
In quest of wisdom, admitting foolishness
With Thanks, knowing that
   offering gratitude brings fortitude
With yearning to be in His Grace

What about riches?

***Amma* would answer:**

There are no better riches than
   acceptance of Life as it is
Doing what you can do best
Resilience to withstand all hurdles
Good health to meet
   the purpose of every day
Wisdom to differentiate
   between right and wrong

Being humble and grateful
　　in His Compassionate Grace

With a twinkle in her eyes,
***Amma* would add:**

Do not hanker, despise greed
Let other riches seek you
And remember always
You get what you deserve
Only when it becomes due

~*~

Let us pray
Amma's way

Love yourself
by being true to yourself
Be not in haste to react
First anticipate then contemplate
and
then respond
Follow the right path
Be happy
Be successful.

Cyclical

The cycle
of physical birth and death
    despite variance
    amongst different species
remains a subset
of a larger cycle of Nature

In the journey of
the human cycle
from birth to death
we are busy
producing, consuming,
acquiring, dumping
creating, procreating
building, destroying
    … and rebuilding …
eventually
leaving something behind
good, bad, or ugly
for the next generation
to inherit.

What is bestowed
reflects
individuality
in the form of
achievements or failures

within the governing
norms and customs
of the social environs
where the individual lived.

Such is the game plan
of *Prakriti* and *Purusha*
that innumerable civilizations
have come and gone
and man is still wandering
here, there, everywhere
in understanding
the greater cycle of Nature.

Is it all pre-scripted?

Or, perhaps, it is
the gravitational pull and push
eternally perpetuating
in the cosmos
with its own
systematic
yet incomprehensible plan
encompassing all laws
of physics and chemistry
in the form of
Sattva, *Rajas* and *Tamas*

as the trinity
of creation, sustenance and destruction
manifesting eternally
from the unknown Energy
that has countless names

No wonder
Amma called this
a mere play
the inexorable *Leela*

Quest

If life is cyclical
a mere play
an inexorable *Leela*

Then

What is this phenomenon
of recurring births and deaths
that the Scriptures talk about?
What is Salvation
that everyone wants to attain?

I asked Amma.

Amma replied:

While being physically alive
everyone goes through
      without volition
millions of microscopic cycles
of the birth and death marvel

Most remain oblivious to this wonder

What? I asked perplexed

***Amma* explained:**

In between the heartbeats
       incarnating birth and death
is the tiny space
encapsulating the cosmos
where *Life* lives majestically
in myriad forms and impulses

Remember,
Life is in the Now
of cause and effect
Not in the past nor in the future

Be *Silent* and *Listen**
To what *Life* wants to say
Meditate on the experience
Get not attached
Simply immerse
Become the Witness
Relax

Then? I asked overwhelmed

***Amma* went on:**

Then
There will be
Nothing more to know
Nothing to gain, nothing to Lose

All conceptual debates
of birth, death, cycles, salvation
known and unknown
will adjourn and merge
in the abyss of silence

The *Leela* will march on
with the vibrance and radiance
of its own glory

***Amma* suggested:**

Try it!

... and the quest goes on ...

* Simply rearranged, the alphabets used to write "Silent"
and "Listen" are same. Perhaps to listen comprehensively
one must indeed be truly silent.

Word

Amma spent
a lot of time
with us…

When I, my siblings
and cousins were
growing up, once
during our summer
get-together, *Amma*
came up with an idea.

She said:

Close your eyes
Visualize water
Concentrate
        … silence
                a brief gap …
Now narrate
What unfolds?

I started describing
momentarily experienced
streams of images

Jal, Water, thirst,
clouds, lightning, thunder,
rain, shower, brook,

spring, well, lake, pond,
river, fish, turtles, swimming,
Dams, floods, tides, ocean ...

Oh yes, bathing,
washing, cooking,
cleaning, hygiene, laundry ...
And of course,
liquids, juices, fruits
sweet, sour, tasty,
and my favorite
summer delight
... the watermelons.

And I stopped ... gasping for breath

***Amma* mused**:

See how a word reveals!

Be it any word
its several layers
concealed within
connect to other words
forever expanding
as the tree of life
Of all the images
whatever allures most

reflects personal affections
hence get entertained
and stirred in the mind
transforming into a dream,
fantasy, an aspiration,
an aim, a goal or target,
purpose to achieve
friends to play
lover to embrace
enemy to squash
song to sing
rhythm for dance
to stay healthy, happy
and in harmony

Just one word
and so much learnt
Imagine if one contemplates
on the Word of words;
would not one
get the key to unlock
the supreme potential within,
that encapsulates
the absolute existence

Mesmerized since,
I am still overwhelmed

Amma

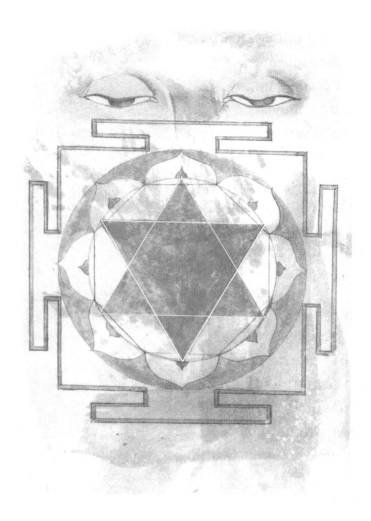

Amma's lullabies:
Surely reminiscent to-date
those devotional vibes
even today consecrate

Amma's nurturing:
Grow beyond the parent
become wise and strong
be alive, to live with aplomb

Amma's *parathas*:
An unforgettable taste
reminding to chew good
not to be eaten in haste

Amma's command:
Face the bully squarely
settle scores outside
before returning home

Amma's family:
Love, by being true to yourself
become capable to envelope
everyone in your embrace

Amma's generosity:
Feel rich by sharing -
Life bequeaths aplenty
to the one full of caring

Amma's spirituality:
Love yourself immensely
forgiving upon realization
the involuntary errors

Amma's mysticism:
Death is inevitable
sleep with gratitude
for the ultimate dawn

Love yourself
by being true to yourself
Be not in haste to react
First anticipate then contemplate
and
then respond
Follow the right path
Be happy
Be successful.

Caring

When I was growing up
Amma was my favorite
the dependable refuge

Always poised carrying
an angelic smile, she met
with wide-open arms

Ever ready to embrace
sending feelings of safety
imparting lavish confidence

Her gestures reinforced
a sense of belonging
and caring commitment

Formulating a guidance of
unifying the triad of aspiration,
inspiration, and perspiration

To engross in the process
of activity, and cherish the
virtue of the work well-done

Healing

Ever since *Corona*
raised its ghostly head
for a ghostly dance
to the pandemonium tunes,
causing death and disruption,
everyone is anxious.

Exasperated and helpless,
seeking refuge,
I have invoked *Amma,*
several times, wondering,
how she would have dealt
with the uncertain situation

Each time,
Amma's gospel
resonates therapeutically:

> Always remember
> but fear not *Yama*
> for death is inevitable

> Know and follow *Yam*
> the *Patanjali sutras*
> of self-control

> The situation demands
> rigorous discipline
> more than ever before.

I hear *Amma* reiterating:
Love yourself
by being true to yourself.

~*~

The *sutras* are aphorisms –

TO BE:
clean, committed, content,
honest, kind, loyal, non-violent,
persevering, poised and tolerant,

and

NOT TO BE:
a cheat, greedy or a thief.

Love yourself
by being true to yourself
Be not in haste to react
First anticipate then contemplate
and
then respond
Follow the right path
Be happy
Be successful.

Connection

Her deep eyes talk
conveying much to hear
whenever I see her fading
sepia image from years ago

I simply strive to decipher
and then try finding words
to articulate what is heard
in the serenity of her silence

Esteem

He barked, she heard
Her silence, he felt
Intrigued, he quizzed
She remained quiet

To her the respect for
the precepts of dignity
was far more important
than winning an argument

Maturity

Whenever she talked
it was a gracious expression
Her pensive feelings
were lovingly understood

That what remained unsaid
was her unpretentiousness,
Deeply etched by an
invisible level of discretion

Compassion

The folks rooted to
unity of family values
do understand that
the charity of kindness,
tolerance and love,
begins at home

Those who don't, end up
in malicious antagonism
first destroying themselves,
then the families, extending
to clans, friends, societies
and even nations.

Destination

My father always said:

I held your hand
and taught you to walk;
One day
when you will become a father
you too will do the same

But remember always
to simply emulate
not to replicate,
for my guidance
is merely a path
not the destination

With the
changing times
paths also change
and if you discover
a different and progressive path
to reach the destination
simply discard mine

Impose not on your children
your footprints, rules and criterion
simply lend them
a helping hand
that's full of true love and motivation

so that they experience Freedom
to walk on a path
that will lead them
to the destination

Parenting is nothing
but a path
which changes
generation after generation
but never the destination.

The destination
always is emancipation
of the Self.

Love yourself
by being true to yourself
Be not in haste to react
First anticipate then contemplate
and
then respond
Follow the right path
Be happy
Be successful.

Poise

One who knows how,
when and what to speak,
where and why to be quiet,
in all humility grows strong
to reign the wild horses
galloping in mind's racecourse.

Such a proficiency allows
the whispers of the conscience,
to be clearly heard with
a clarity of risk and reward,
for wise execution of actions
in every pursuit of life

It trashes deranged impressions
that cause distressful delusions

Shiva

River in tresses
Flames in eye
Nectar on crescent
Poison in throat
Ashes on body
Revelry with ghosts …

Necklet Serpent
Cosmic Trident
Energy vibrating
Damru pulsating

Images rivaling
Forces opposing
Typify diversity
Coexisting alive by
The union divine of
The dancing *Nataraja*

Patience

No matter what
needs to be done
warrants performance
with humility, attention
and caring commitment

akin to the devotion
of *Nandi* the bull
sitting outside
the *Shiva* temple
with intense forbearance

Today

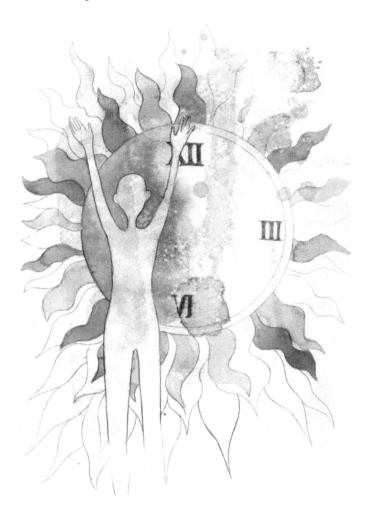

Today
is inimitably
a wonderful day

Recapitulating
continuation and
the fragility of life

Bequeathing one more
opportunity to appreciate
what is *now* before us

Affirming there is not
another better reason
to experience life

The Present

Before cognition happens
or expression takes place
Now − the moment
      slips away
another chapter gets added
to the epoch of life

Bound
in the limits of
Time, Space and Causation
The perception of *the present*
      the natural gift from God
remains perpetually camouflaged
within the diurnal shades

Transcend the limits;
eliminate the shadows
and experience
Now as Eternity...

So, proclaim the Masters
When will I learn
to venerate the gift?

Now

Plausibly
the *real* now
is a giant void
or a black hole
sucking in the future
simultaneously
converting it into a past,
to be dreaded or glorified,
to satiate one's own
intellectual perceptions
and beliefs

Life is effectively lived
learning, good or bad,
from the past
and either worrying
or dreaming about
the distant future

Alas!
The present that
is apparently
witnessing and
experiencing
remains elusive.

How does one
truly come
face to face
with *now*
that seems to be
a fleeting moment
yet *is* an eternity
in itself?

Love yourself
by being true to yourself
Be not in haste to react
First anticipate then contemplate
and
then respond
Follow the right path
Be happy
Be successful.

Unpredictable

Unpredictable, yet wonderful
is the swinging grandeur of life
ecstatic in *her* own majestic play
dancing mysteriously and luring
with inexplicable melodies, that

cajole, seduce entice, mystify,
enthrall, captivate, mesmerize,
tempt, coax, coerce, deceive,
embrace, accept, resist, reject,
form, sustain and destroy;

creating a complex engaging riddle,
to ensure that man, *ad infinitum*,
bewildered and overwhelmed,
continues to explore *her* infinite lore
by being a seeker forever ...

Gurdwara

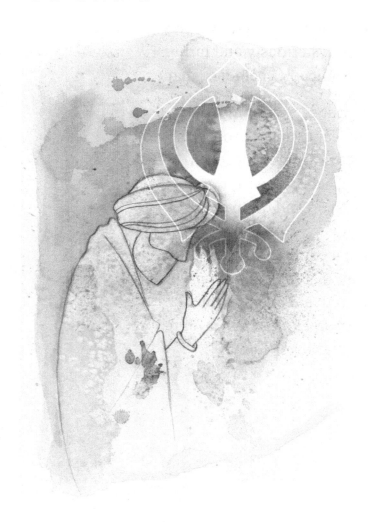

On this side of the gate is *"I"*
On that side of the gate is "Supreme"

The Guru stands at the Gate

Beware of charlatans!

Be alert and cognize
    Fear not,
    because
The True Guru does not spare

The Guru will destroy
your most precious possession
− the Ego

Are you ready?

If yes:

You will cross the Gate (*dwar*)
and become one with the One

"I" will cease
Even the concept of "God"
will disappear

The realization
The attainment
   – will simply be –
the primordial energy
   the sound of the silence

Ik Onkar Satnam*

* One - Primordial Energy - Supreme Truth
Ik Onkar Satnam are the first three words
of the *Mulmantra* (the prologue) of
Guru Nanak's *Japji Sahib*

Love yourself
by being true to yourself
Be not in haste to react
First anticipate then contemplate
and
then respond
Follow the right path
Be happy
Be successful.

Steps

First step
marks the onset
of journey

Every next step
taken gracefully
 with dignified integrity
 loving empathy
 faithful fortitude
 courageous forbearance
intuitively transforms
the chosen path into
precise direction

Notwithstanding
the challenges
 of seasonal warnings
 social rebukes
 fluctuating doubts
 knocks and bumps
encountered
in between

Awesome
is the experience
once the mindful
grasps the proximity
to the destination

~*~

Keep going
The end is close

Jai Ho!

Love yourself
by being true to yourself
Be not in haste to react
First anticipate then contemplate
and
then respond
Follow the right path
Be happy
Be successful.

Devotion

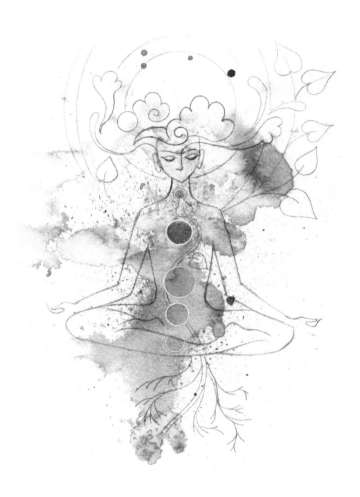

The One beyond infinity
permeating the cosmos
is mystically invisible

The brush fails to draw
and the lexicon fails
miserably to articulate

Yet the unspoken
forms bridges
of interaction

With unwitting links of
sighs, smiles, laughs
and flowing tears

This contented sanity
or mindless inanity
are enigmatic wits

Being in obeisance,
one gets fulfilled with
overflowing bliss

Nature

An inherent marvel
of illusory chaos
is the logic of nature
where Earth rotating on its
own axis revolves around
the relatively unmoving Sun

This perpetual motion creates
the circadian routine of
day and night
as an eternal recurrence
thereby manifesting
Life of cyclic seasons in
the pairs of opposites

Love and hate
heaven and hell
joy and sorrow
birth and death ...
as the obverse and reverse
of the same coin

One is amazed by this duality
as the singularity of Oneness
that the Gurus talk about

The Mystic

Bookworm may miss
the undertones of words
written or articulated;
The mystic hears the silence

Impromptu and biased
reactions come freely
from pseudo critics;
The mystic remains calm

Egoist must argue
ferociously to prove a point
concealing guilt and greed;
The mystic wisely smiles

Youth dynamically acts
as go-getter vibrant
exercising will power;
The mystic conquers all

Desire compels learning
to accumulate something;
The mystic by unlearning
evolves to arrive at nothing

Impetus

Those responsible
for elbowing
problematic conditions,
are in fact Godsent catalysts,
steadily triggering
the sparks of motivation

Recognizing such impetus,
one who doesn't get daunted, but
accepts the surfacing challenges
and strives dedicatedly
to overcome the obstacles,
is actually the true *Karma Yogi*

Life

Life is the only constant
that is forever changing

This four-letter word
    encompassing dynamic vibrance
    mysteriously challenging
when meditated upon
unfolds exclusively
to extrapolate distinctively
the individual perception
as a prize or penalty
with a unique portrayal every time
illustrating the experience
of transformation
within and without

Contemplate and transcend
by discovering
the essence of Life

~*~

Here are some connotations:

    Labor is finest endeavor
    Lacuna is forever emptiness
    Last is first exiting
    Lambast is fiery emotion
    Lamenting is foolish endeavor

Lapse is failure expired
Laughter is funny exercise
Less is fairly enriching
Lethargic is forfeiting enthusiasm
Lethargy is fortifying errors
Life is fairly easy
Life is for everyone
Life is furtively enigmatic
Light idea forceful energy
Live in full enlightenment
Live intelligently feel emancipated
Lively idea focused end
Lively inside fully energized
Longing inside food excites
Lonely inside fuels enigma
Loneliness is forfeiting ecstasy
Loot is fraudulent extra
Lore is folk education
Lose individuality fracture ego
Lost in futile effort
Love ignites fiery excitement
Love involves fundamental energy
Love is fondly energizing
Love is fantastic experience
Love is forgiving endlessly
Lust is filthy encroachment

~*~

… and
notwithstanding the inferences
Life - the eternal mystic
moves on
with its own conundrum
of paradoxes, riddles, puzzles
in myriad hues
of vagaries and variables.

Transient

Anything that can be
seen and touched
is a mere configuration
of the elements five

Everything that can be
measured, weighed, and counted,
is constitutionally subject
to eventual annihilation

So, all that exists
is an experience of
the forever changing body
of Life itself in transit

It is ominously catastrophic
for the whimpers that negate,
but for the lively and carefree
it is a reason to celebrate

Do it

The youngest wondering
What and why to do it
The jobless youth
Clueless, how to do it

The middle-aged frustrated
Too busy, no time to do it
The Octogenarians mumble
No need to do it

Unable to manage the
pandemic and social distancing
The bemused leaders thunder
Don't talk, just do it

Independence

Comprehend
Space, Air, Water, Fire, Earth
to be aware of
the dependence of all
on these elements
to acquire a form

Offer gratitude to all
known and unknown
past and present
as without being
dependent on them
one cannot get
essentials to live
and celebrate life

Surrender in all humility
to the Witness within
the only Sovereign
unperturbed and carefree
as the eternal concept
of independence

Observation

Functional basics are sacred and
have remained unchanged ever since
humans started walking on earth

Earth's landscape, every few miles,
changes topography, stimulating
social, cultural, and dialectic distinction.

Everyone knows, acknowledges,
and admires the obvious differences
with proclamation of *unity in diversity*:

a rational and wise declaration.
It is, perhaps, a pre-requisite
for the evolutionary growth of man.

Yet, the edict is repeatedly betrayed
and threatened to be destroyed
by mankind's identity crisis.

History is replete with brutal acts
exploiting the peculiarities with
prejudice, hate and manipulation.

The trend continues even today,
to desecrate the *Garden of Eden*
in the name of One *unknown* God.

Is this a permanent strategy devised
by a few warlords who use exploitation
and tyranny to play the power games?

One questions if there is something
more disgraceful known to mankind
besides the cruel and beastly instincts?

No wonder, the mystic wanders!

Love yourself
by being true to yourself
Be not in haste to react
First anticipate then contemplate
and
then respond
Follow the right path
Be happy
Be successful.

Maya

That
what was not
    yesterday
but is
    today
and will not be
    tomorrow

If it is not trickery
— an illusion —
then what is it?

Leaf

The Autumn saw
my green body turn yellow
and with the flow of winds
I moved on towards
my new journey.

The tree, my father
having nurtured me
standing majestically
and silently
did not hold me anymore.

I had come of age
capable to embrace
the dew drops
and dance with
the blades of grass

Eventually to become dust
and dissolve into
the eternal embrace
of Mother earth

Is this dissolution
Death or Life?
Perhaps, the path
that we seek ... Nirvana

Detachment

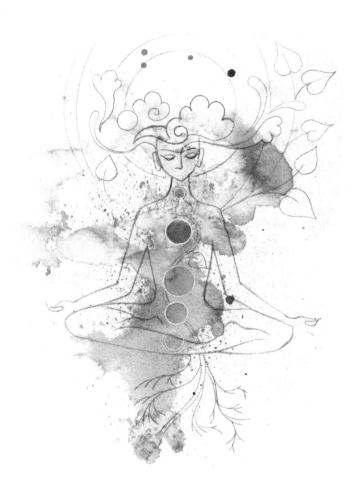

Detachment is
the ability to switch off
   disconnect at will
from any action and simply be
with the self within
relaxing and enjoying
the greatest magical show
of the moment
by being still and silent

Listen ably the vibes
to grasp the message
that reveals the when,
where, how and why
of what ought to be done
to nurture the roots,
and rejuvenated, fulfil
the purpose of one's life

Whatever that blueprint may be,
accept with gratitude and humility
execute and grow with it in harmony
for the *Karmic* dynamism
needs to remain carefree

Heaven and Hell

Reaching home
after days drudgery ...

If welcomed with
hugs and smiles
sweet home is the heaven
reflecting one's virtues
and good deeds

Instead, if nagged
and neglected -
wretched hell is the house
mirroring one's cruelty
immorality and misdeeds

Both heaven and hell
are echoes and images
revealing the temperament
of one's own persona

Guilt

Activity is inherent
so long as one is alive
Ensure no action causes
guilty regrets in life

Shame, infamy, disgrace, are
the devils that sting the soul
penance, repentance, apology
do temporary damage control

Repudiation

Gains attained by
subjugation, suppression,
plotting or fixing
for selfish ends
do not stay long, and
degrade equanimity

History reveals
opulent royals
and sundry corrupt,
confined in their closets,
dreadfully wrestling
with their own malevolence,
having failed miserably
to call their soul as own

Amma insisted:
Renounce deceit
Shun crookedness

Musing

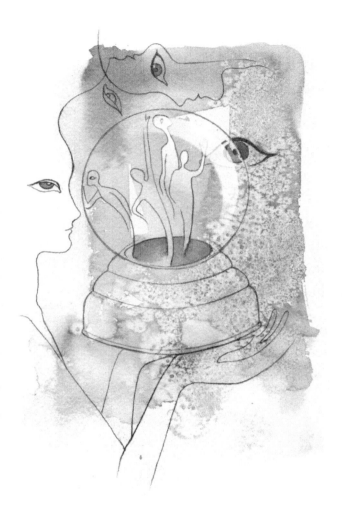

Be a focused observer
and watch objectively,
the ants' pageantry
pacing and tracing
routes and terrains
One will discover
a shared network
capable and united
to overcome hurdles
arising in their sites.

Write notable points
then adjudge the scroll,
delete the superfluous,
sanctify and validate
the final note

The idea will emerge
lively and worthy
to be awarded the verdict,
as an ideology,
to pursue and explore
While the pageantry,
in all its grandeur,
continues parading
the exalted lifestyle
and regime of unity

Purpose

Whatever the vocation
crossroads appear
offering conflicting options

However baffling,
it is the underlying reason
that inspires or dissuades

Altruistic aim propels
legitimate constructive efforts
Vanity induces fraudulency

Plausibly, the cause itself
genetically engineers
and begets the path

That gets invariably opted
for better or worse
as the *karmic* seed

Sown today to sprout tomorrow
into a fruit deserved
as the prize or punishment

Renunciation

As one ages
the decaying body
brings to focus
the fragility of life

Realization dawns,
withdrawal commences
from the messy rivalries
and greedy ambitions

Accepting with gratitude
whatever life bequeaths
to become burden free
of all likes and dislikes

One, fearless of any loss
or worrisome of any gain
immerses in pure relaxation,
until the vacation is over

Love yourself
by being true to yourself
Be not in haste to react
First anticipate then contemplate
and
then respond
Follow the right path
Be happy
Be successful.

Previews

Of Memories Wisdom and Benediction

Certain life-forms never perish!

They continue to speak to their seekers across the intervening thick veil of time and space; solidity of the physicality and after-stage; a disembodied voice heard distinctly from some deep place; a being of other dimensionalities, locations, realms telecommunicating from another medium - the other side of living, this time, as transformed energies of another type.

Rajender Krishan, a successful New York-based Indian-American, faced with the existential dilemmas, seeks out his *Amma ji* who, according to his candid confession elsewhere in this great collection of poems, continues to guide him in her own grandmotherly way from the great beyond.

Now the poet in him wishes to share the gained insights with readers of a new-millennium world grappling with the harsh political realities and truths that can be very unsettling for the believers of ethics and liberal democracy as framing narratives of the civilizational functionality and progress. Even otherwise, many challenges come up during a short human journey on the *terra firma* - and when existing frameworks fail to enthuse and guide the daily conduct of society and individual, answers are sought to the same by a mind trying for solace and resolution.

This illustrated book of heart-felt moments of queries provides some answers in a lyrical form that has got its own flow, pace and internal rhythm. Mini gems. Nuggets of inspiring words from a man rooted in his heritage and inclined towards spiritual aspects of the phenomena, exploration of every side of the lived experience.

Rajender Krishan is free of academic paraphernalia - of the heavy burden of theories and schools - and comes across as a refreshing voice in an age of the FB poetry where, sadly, anything goes unlegislated, in the name of free verse and blank poetry - words strung together, at their best, and eminently forgettable, like a viral video, tweet and Instagram image. Perhaps, it is designed for that only.

RK's offerings are deceptively simple in such a landscape - but, in reality, very profound!

His poetry challenges collective amnesia imposed by a media society that tries to dumb down culture and its expression through art.

Here, certain deep truths are discussed with the ease of a Zen artist.

Take a look, please, at this observation by a grandmother in blissful mood:

In between the heartbeats
*　　　incarnating birth and death*
is the tiny space
encapsulating the cosmos
where Life lives majestically
in myriad forms and impulses

Remember,
Life is in the Now
of cause and effect
Not in the past nor in the future

Be Silent and Listen
To what Life wants to say
Meditate on the experience
Get not attached
Simply immerse
Become the Witness
Relax.

Amma's Gospel is full of startling comments about mysteries of life, death, cessation, rebirth of different kinds...and of charged words that have got a strange luminosity of their own through interaction with Holy Scriptures and point to a rightful conduct.

After reading these poems, the reader feels fulfilled, elevated and revived!

And that is the primary task of any philosophy and art - change to a higher form of cognition.

It is epistemological poetics in its basic impact and overall affect administered subtly on the recipient consciousness - a poetry that guides as a treasure trove of wisdom and divine benediction.

Poetry and philosophy; morality and aesthetics crossed.

It is life talking to you through a wise woman and a respectful listener in a remembering/seeking mode, of a presence in an absence, capturing the fleet-footed moments, dialogues, in verse - words spring forth like a new spring from an aching heart.

Of memories and their enduring relevance.
Of past in the present; present in the past.

Of seeking a guru - and getting the right answers.
Of a grandmother, dead/living:

Her deep eyes talk
conveying much to hear
whenever I see her fading
sepia image from years ago

I simply strive to decipher
and then try finding words
to articulate what is heard
in the serenity of her silence

Read - and get enlightened!

It is sheer meditation!

– Sunil Sharma, Educator, Writer, Critic, Mumbai

Rare Pearl

Each poem in *Amma*'s Gospel is a rare pearl, an outcome of the wisdom and knowledge of sages in the scriptures – churned, filtered through experience, chiseled, and wrapped with the novelty of vocabulary for the benefit of humanity. Written during the ongoing Covid-19 pandemic, Rajender Krishan comes out with crystal clear understanding of life's complexities by rising to higher realms by recalling *Amma* meditatively.

In nutshell, *Amma* ji is a guiding pole star, a teacher, a universal motherly figure ready to hold hands to navigate through the labyrinth of life.

– Neera Pradhan, Lecturer and Counsellor, Bhubaneswar

Spirituality and Devotion

Our religion is based on a tradition, a cautious and deliberately considered system. The common beginning of a sacred prayer is *maatru devo bhava, pitrudevo bhava, aacharyadevo bhava and atidhi devo bhava.* This has started in human beings since time immemorial.

The first reading of *Amma's Gospel* makes us think of the 17th Century Blaise Pascal, and his *Pensées* and Rochefoucauld's *Maxims*. Those and the contemporary poet think deep and with great inward looking. The thought processes of all the three are the same, or at least, alike.

Spirituality and faith go hand in hand. These are followed in accordance with the rules and instruction laid down by parents and most importantly by their mothers. Hence the paramount guidance of mother, *maa*. Children follow obeying the mother.

This short, but most important book, is the penning of the thought processes which whirl round the Mother. Reading it thoughtfully and slowly we are sure to look within and around, scaling heights of devotion and higher ways and ideal principles of life and living.

Rajender's constant confabulations in *Amma's Gospel* lead us in the proper direction.

– Dr. Rama Rao Vadapalli, VB, Author, Solapur.

Love yourself
by being true to yourself
Be not in haste to react
First anticipate then contemplate
and
then respond
Follow the right path
Be happy
Be successful.

Timeless Wisdom

Amma who inspired these poems is an inheritor of the timeless wisdom of womanhood, the strength of eternal India and the compassion that flows out of our soul if only we can still for a few moments our minds, obsessed with chasing the world outside. Her wisdom could be found in every poem. It is not *Amma* teaching her grandson but the bygone ages imparting their wisdom to an age that has lost its touch with the wisdom of the Oversoul.

The Gospel that begins with an invocation to *Om* and ends in *Renunciation* is a journey into the ageless wisdom of the land where the Vedas and the Upanishads were born, a land that has since their times passed through the blazing fire of much suffering which has remolded that wisdom into nuggets of everyday intelligence that make life worthy of the sacred source from which it has emanated.

– Prof. Satya Chaitanya, Educator and Corporate Trainer, Jamshedpur.

Universal and Timeless Nuggets of Wisdom!

'*Amma's* Gospel' contains the essence of all the values inherited by the poet, Shri Rajender Krishan from his paternal grandmother, which have Universal and Timeless significance. The neatly packed forty and five poems filled with rhythm, aesthetics, intensity and imagery accompanied by luminous illustrations are loving gifts for posterity. The poems filled with hope and traditional Indian values, which constitute the wisdom of the great sages over the ages are sure to guide the youth growing up in a beleaguered and tense world filled with much animosity, sickness, confusion and lack of compassion to face the challenges of life and march on the right path.

– Dr. S. Padmapriya, PhD, Academician, Author, Bengaluru

Amma Personified

Rajender Krishan has very aptly christened the book as "*Amma's Gospel*", indicative of the sacred knowledge conveyed through 45 poems. Simple and devout Amma ji reminds me of Lord Krishna when among the many other life lessons, she tells her young and vulnerable grandson to 'Face the bully squarely, settle scores outside before returning home'. Similarly, her impeccable faith is reflected when she says, 'The One that is always with me; Have no doubt, That One Knows'. *Amma*'s life is a paradigm of true knowledge and ethical living.

I thoroughly enjoyed reading the book.

– Dr. Jaipal Singh, Educator, Bureaucrat, Corporate Advisor, Lucknow

Amma Belongs to All

Rajender Krishan's book of poems, *Amma's Gospel* is special, its contents touches the many heavens we aspire, the celestial truth, our mothers have instilled within us. During those turbulent times of 1947, it was *Amma* who steered Rajenderji's family to safety in Delhi and enriched them with understanding, forgiveness and awareness of knowing the self. Each one of us has an *Amma* within us deeply embedded which comes to our rescue in sickness and unhappiness. The *Amma* is the spiritual entity claiming the heart and mind in our journey on earth. The mind and space of the human are the realms where the ancestral spirit lives, making the aura enveloping and protecting the human body even while sleeping and unaware in our daily lives. Rajenderji's *Amma* belongs to all of us, in galaxies where we all finally merge, in her supreme kindness she is dispersed bringing happiness and sanity to all humankind.

– Dr. Amitabh Mitra, Trauma Surgeon /Poet, East London, SA

Amma's Heartbeat

A great being once said "a mystic sees nothing but god." Reading *Amma's Gospel*, I felt a true gem glowing with hints of god. As I contemplated on the verses, I felt *Amma*'s warm presence embrace me and slowly and delightfully, her gentle wisdom surfaced, like an invisible smile beneath the words, tenderly whispering the eternal truth - *Ek Onkar*. And as I allowed Rajender's beautiful visions to illuminate me, they lead me into that one silence where all search for meaning disappears, into the ever-present now - *Amma*'s heartbeat.

This is the power of Rajender's poetry. He takes you straight to your heart, to you. As words become consciousness within, you experience the reality, *Amma* and he are pointing at - *Love yourself by being true to yourself.* *Amma*'s *Gospel* is precious. It is full of wonder, simplicity and harmony, revealing timeless secrets of the self. Written like *sutras*, Rajender's illuminations inspire devotion and silence. Here the soul is free to discover its reasons to be.

– Simi Nallaseth, Film Writer/ Director, Mumbai.

Relevant Guidance

It was the chore of our mothers and grandmothers of yore, who would open their trunk full of folklore laden with sacred wisdom of the sages to shape the moral consciousness and teach the children with "relevant guidance" about dealing with basic human conflicts, desires and relationships in a truthful way. *Amma's Gospel* does exactly that by passing on the "pearls of wisdom" that Rajender imbibed from *Amma ji*.

This collection is a must-read as each poem is a revelation, a source of life lessons and cultural values. Like a religious scripture, the more one reads, the more one can find pointers that can shape one's personality positively.

– Rajiv Khandelwal, Entrepreneur, Author, Poet, Agra.

Homage to Amma

Corona forced social isolation has made people depressed, anxious with surges in mental health concerns. But Rajender with this collection of poems has shared another aspect, where the downtime became a creative time by channeling it for a poetic endeavor. In an amazingly short period of time we have witnessed unfolding of geyser of flow from his heart, which he captured on paper as homage to *Amma*. The wise words of his grandmother – *Amma*, helped the child in his growth and development, and now words of that grownup child, in the form of this bouquet of poetic collection from a grateful heart is a devotional offering steeped in awe, constitutes a homage to *Amma*.

– Bhupinder Singh, author of *Humility: A Spiritual Journey and Why Are We Here?* Houston

About the Poet

Born in 1951, Rajender Krishan (*aka* Raj Chowdhry), the editor of Boloji, got education in Bal Bharati and Air Force School, and after matriculation from PU, Chandigarh, completed graduation from Delhi University. He has extensive experience in poultry farming, advertising, sales and marketing, antique reproductions and real estate consultancy. In 1989, he migrated to New York, USA with his wife Meera Chowdhry and two children.

Now, a grandfather, Rajender Krishan believes in the freedom of expression and is an admirer of *Kabir*. He is passionate about Poetry, Photography and Visual Art. He loves to share his thoughts with hundreds of writers – poets, journalists, novelists, critics and artists through his website **Boloji.com** that he started in 1999.

Boloji.COM

Since 1999, Boloji.com has been an open platform, showcasing the work of amateur and professional writers from all over the world, including eminent novelists, poets, journalists, doctors and more.

Do you want to Boloji?
We are listening.

www.boloji.com

Made in the USA
Middletown, DE
14 November 2020

966060R00096